This book is dedicated to
my mother, Mary, and her
most recent husband, Larry.

This may sound as though my mother goes through husbands like Elizabeth Taylor. She does not. She was married to my father for 25 years, widowed for ten, and along came Larry. She will be accepting applications for her next husband in the spring of 2017.

Preface

"It was twenty years ago today, Sgt. Pepper taught the band to play." That was what everyone was singing fifteen years ago when I published my first book of poetry. The year was 1967 and I was seventeen. Half my lifetime later people are still playing Sgt. Pepper, and I'm still at it.

I'm not at it with the same, uh, youthful enthusiasm I had when I began. At 32 I don't seem to be falling in love as often as I did when I was seventeen. Early on I was turning out two books and two relationships a year. This is my first book of poetry since 1978's *Come To My Senses*, and that was my first book since 1974.

Fifteen years is not a major anniversary. People celebrate ten years of something with a certain enthusiasm, then everything is relatively quiet until the 25th year. (We had a ten-year high school reunion in 1977. This year I didn't even get a post card.)

I guess I'm supposed to say something like, "It doesn't *seem* like fifteen years," but it does. Fifteen years seems about right. I'm entirely different, and yet I'm completely the same. To quote the Beatles again,

"Oh bla de, Oh bla da, life goes on. Lordy, how that life goes on."

Thank you for reading this book.

Take care,

Peter

West Hollywood, California
May, 1982

This book published by
Prelude Press
Box 69773
Los Angeles, California
90069

The illustrations for this book were taken from the Dover Pictorial Archive Series. A catalog of their books is available from Dover Publications, 180 Varick Street, New York, New York 10014.

LOVE POEMS

Fresh love.
First poem.
Inspiration.
Joy.

Tee hee.

here
you were,
dancing.

I saw only your back at first.
Then a hint of your profile.
But even then I knew
my search had found
in you a fulfilment.

The long search.

The search I would abandon,
and then realize that the search
included that abandonment.

There
you were,
dancing.

I am not
a total
stranger.

I am a
perfect
stranger.

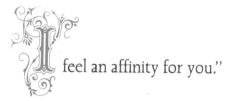 feel an affinity for you."

I guess that's as close
as clever people ever
come to saying
"I love you."

On the first date.

m I mad?

Am I remarkably lonely
or remarkably perceptive?

How can I be feeling such caring
and tenderness and devotion?

How can I be feeling this
so soon? How have I lasted
without it so long?

It is a risk to love.

What if it doesn't
work out?

Ah,
but what if it does.

This whole lifetime spent
growing and learning and
risking and failing and
succeeding and selecting
and gathering and preparing.

I had begun to wonder:
What is all this for?

And now comes the answer,

You.

Every time I do
something wonderful
I immediately think
of sharing it with you.

Gosh, love.

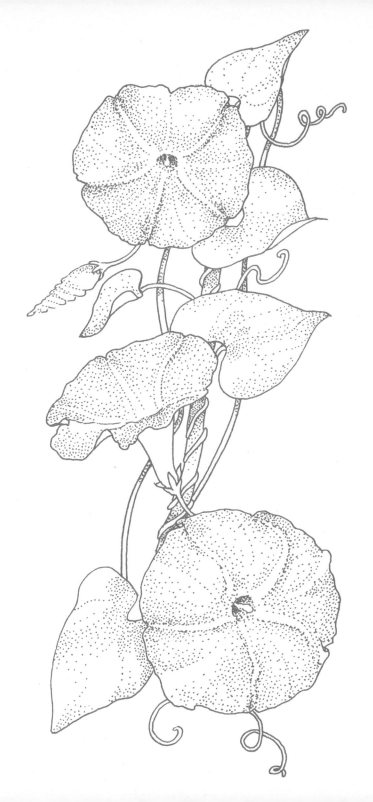

he longing
The laughing
The loving
The living

The joy
The pain
The sun
The rain.

Thank you.

I'm in love again.

Everyone sighs at
sunsets and roses.

I sigh at
sunsets and roses
and you.

irports. Cabs. Hotels. Airports. Rent-a-cars. Airports.

This world is not very real.

Sometimes only the memory of you keeps me going.

I await the reality of your embrace.

You
are the nicest
thing I could
ever do for
myself.

erfect joy and
perfect sorrow.

One following another
following another.

The poles, the extremes,
of emotional life and
all points in between.

Following one another.
Following one another.

Gently up, gently down,
like the ocean under a boat.

What a wonderful
place this is,
loving you.

don't know whether
I want you because I love you
or
I love you because I want you.

Which came first, the chicken
or Colonel Sanders?

I do know that I
love being with you and
I like thinking about you.

My love is with you this day.

This poem
is a kiss
for your mind.

Life is
not a
struggle.

It's a
wiggle.

Rose

 hy do I
think of
Christmas
when I see
a rose?

Is it the
red and the green
or is it the
love?

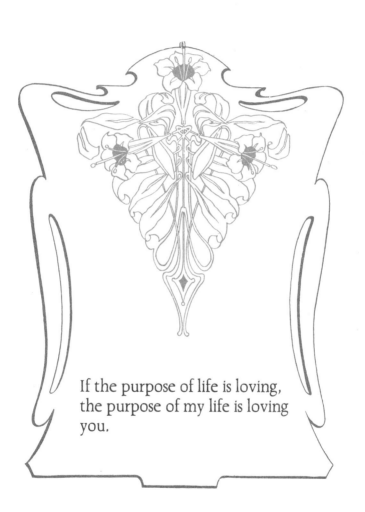

If the purpose of life is loving,
the purpose of my life is loving
you.

oes the earth
have a sky
or
does the sky
have an earth?

Does the body
have an aura
or
does the aura
have a body?

Do we have love
or
does love have us?

I've heard a lot
about the dangers of
living beyond one's means.

What worries me, however,
is my current habit of
living beyond my meanings.

The difference between
love and loving

is the difference between
fish and fishing.

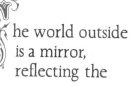he world outside
is a mirror,
reflecting the

good & bad
joy & sorrow
laughter & tears

within me.

Some people are
difficult mirrors
to look into,

but you....

I look at you
and I see
all the beauty
inside of me.

My love and
God's Light
be with you

in all that
you are and
in all that
you do.

row
row
row
romance,

gently down the
stream. merrily,
merrily, merrily,
marry me. life
is but a dream.

Some of Peter McWilliams' books
are available by mail.
Mostly poetry, they are

Come Love With Me & Be My Life

For Lovers & No Others

I Love Therefore I am

The Hard Stuff: Love

Love: An Experience Of

Love is Yes

Come to My Senses

How to Survive the Loss of a Love

And, mostly not poetry

The Word Processing Book: A Short Course in Computer Literacy

The first seven books listed (and additional copies of this book) are
$4.95 each. *How to Survive the Loss of a Love* is $2.95. *The Word Processing
Book* (all about using computers, rather than typewriters, to write
with) is $8.95.

All books can be ordered by mail. Please include $1.00 with each
order for postage and handling.

Prelude Press
5806 Elizabeth Court
Allen Park, Michigan
48101

Thank You